Vive la French Toast!

Vive la French Toast!

Text by GAIL GRECO

Photographs by TOM BAGLEY

RUTLEDGE HILL PRESS

Nashville, Tennessee

Published in Nashville, Tennessee, by Rutledge Hill Press, Inc., 211 Seventh Avenue North, Nashville, Tennessee 37219. Distributed in Canada by H.B. Fenn & Company, Ltd., 34 Nixon Road, Bolton, Ontario L7E 1W2. Distributed in Australia by Millennium Books, 33 Maddox Street, Alexandria NSW 2015. Distributed in New Zealand by Tandem Press, 2 Rugby Road, Birkenhead, Auckland 10. Distributed in the United Kingdom by Verulam Publishing, Ltd., 152a Park Street Lane, Park Street, St. Albans, Hertfordshire AL2 2AU.

Photographs by Tom Bagley
Photo art direction and styling by Gail Greco
Food styling assistance by Priscilla Powers and Todd Seidl
Editorial assistance by Tricia Conaty
Cover and book design by Gore Studio, Inc.
Text layout and typesetting by John Wilson Design
All recipes selected and edited for the home kitchen by Gail Greco

ON THE FRONT COVER: FRENCH TOAST SUNDAE AT THE INN AT ROUND BARN FARM,
WAITSFIELD, VERMONT, RECIPE ON PAGE 82
PICTURE FACING TITLE PAGE: BRANDIED CRANBERRY-RICOTTA FRENCH TOAST, RECIPE ON PAGE 66

Greco, Gail.
    Viva la French toast! / Gail Greco ; photography by Tom Bagley.
        p. cm.
    Includes index.
    ISBN 1-55853-435-0
    1. French toast.   2. Bed and breakfast accommodations—United
States—Directories.   I. Title.
TX770.F73G74   1996
641.5'2—dc20   96-30490
                                                  CIP

Printed in the United States of America

1 2 3 4 5 6 7 8 9 — 00 99 98 97 96

For you, Linda, for your resourcefulness and talent at taking something old and seemingly stale and useless, and turning it into a work of art. You might have invented French toast had you been born a few centuries earlier.

Contents

Other Books in This Series

∾o∾

The Test Kitchen for the
Cooking Association of Country Inns

Although all inn recipes are tried-and-true and served at the inns all the time, the recipes in this cookbook have been further verified and tested for accuracy and clarification for the home kitchen.

The cooking seal of approval that accompanies this book, means that every recipe has been tested in kitchens other than the source, and that the association test kitchen has been satisfied that the recipe is proven and worthy of preparing.

The test kitchen is under the leadership of association founder Gail Greco, with Charla Honea and other editors at Rutledge Hill Press assisting. The prestigious list of kitchen testers is as follows:

DAVID CAMPICHE, *Chef/Owner*
The Shelburne Inn • Seaview, Washington

YVONNE MARTIN, *Chef/Owner*
The White Oak Inn • Danville, Ohio

DEBBIE MOSSIMAN, *Chef/Owner*
Swiss Woods • Lititz, Pennsylvania

PATRICK RUNKEL, *Chef/Owner*
October Country Inn • Bridgewater Corners, Vermont

CLAUDIA RYAN, *Chef/Owner*
Windflower Country Inn • Great Barrington, Massachusetts

ELIZABETH TURNEY, *Chef/Owner*
Bear Creek Lodge • Victor, Montana

MARION YADON, *Chef/Owner*
Canyon Villa Bed & Breakfast • Sedona, Arizona

Try our
Delicious

MILK

A
DISTINCTIVE
SATISFYING
FLAVOR

"Lost" Breads Find Mornings to Celebrate

ONCE UPON A TIME French toast was taken for granted—an offhanded breakfast dish that didn't take much thought or preparation time. It got no respect. The results were—well, what they were intended to be—to give new life to stale bread and parade it as something special from the stovetop griddle, and, in earlier times, from the griddle over the open hearth.

My entrée into the French toast world was in the 1950s with a bread most people (with all due respect) would turn their stuffy French noses up at—Arnold Brick Oven Bread. My mother felt this style of white bread (folks weren't big on whole wheat or multi-grain back then) was denser than most other breads available, such as—heaven forbid—Wonder Bread. Wonder Bread was definitely too light and airy to absorb anything—even when a few days old. Mom never approved of serving something stale (and rarely was bread a leftover in our house anyway). So Arnold's had the home-court advantage all those years while I was growing up in the Bronx.

To prepare the French toast, Mom went basically by the book. She bathed the bread slices into eggs that were beaten with a little bit of cream or milk (yolk and all, of course) and fried them in the melted butter she scooped freely into an old black skillet. When the bread had fried to a deep golden brown on both sides (we all frowned over soggy French toast), she slipped the newly coated Arnold's onto serving plates and we added more butter. It was almost ritualistic to slowly pour the thick amber-colored Vermont-Maid

LEFT: BAKING BISCUIT FRENCH TOAST, RECIPE ON PAGE 2

brand syrup out of Mom's favorite ceramic pitcher. We always took turns shaking the cinnamon out as our garnish and flavor enhancer. The cinnamon would float to the surface of the syrup and cascade overtop the bread—like the dust that falls from Sedona, Arizona's red rocks. This made it all the more delicious later when I would rejoice in soaking up the last piece of bread, now overloaded with cinnamon and syrup. With six of us, Mom would go through a whole loaf. And then things changed.

In the very beginning, French toast had humbly emerged from farmhouse kitchens as a resourceful way to use every leftover crumb. Homemade bread perished more quickly since there was no way to freeze or preserve it. Then French toast emerged with a bit more status. The American palate was changing with the availability of more and interesting products. Haute cuisine was in. French toast was no longer just a way to use up stale bread or "lost bread" (*pain perdu*) as the French called it. Home cooks and professional chefs were beginning to experiment with more intoxicating (in some cases literally intoxicating) ways to serve up egg-dipped bread fried—ah—I mean sautéed as the new culinary nomenclature suggested.

New recipes from creative cooks called for marinating the bread overnight and baking it in the oven, or incorporating a variety of fruit juices and other ingredients into the basic egg-and-milk dipping batter. More and more, exotic breads replaced the simple white bread: whole-wheat breads, crusty bread, Jewish challah bread, Italian panettone, brioche or no bread at all—but pound cake. Fancy sauces with brandies and liqueurs and even fancier toppings from toasted-and-glazed orange rinds and edible, crystallized pansies, were giving French toast a new image. How about a French toast tart of apples and pears or a French Toast Sundae with chocolate chips, nuts, and whipped cream? Or, what about stuffing fruity preserves between two slices of bread or carving out a pocket in crusty bread slices for savory French toasts of breakfast meats and cheeses that have nothing to do at all with maple syrup?

French toast has been given a national identity now as a legitimate dish. All French toast recipes are generally easy to prepare and many can be made ahead of time. French toast—even in its newfangled forms—is an entrée you can depend on to impress and satisfy those waiting at the table. French toast is probably served in greatest variety and most frequently at bed-and-breakfast inns where each reinvented *pain perdu* is as unique as the inn itself.

Innkeepers rely on French toast because this ubiquitous dish comes in so many styles that they can change their menu often. In addition, French toast is a recipe for success. It always looks so good—golden brown and charmed with the likes of fresh fruits, nuts, and inventive sauces.

In this book, you will find a French toast recipe for whatever mood you are in. There are even a few recipes from my own imagination. My French toasts

are very different from the ones Mom used to flip and grill in those early days. But you will find a recipe for Peanut-Butter-and-Jelly French Toast Sandwich, calling for Arnold bread. However, no matter what bread I'm using, or style I'm creating, I am still dedicated to making a really special French toast. I have the same reverence Mom had for crowd-pleasing mornings when the cinnamon shaker was all that was needed for *lost breads* to find a reason to celebrate. Long live French toast!

A few comments about this book

In addition to reading all of my tips for fun
and creative French toast, and my entertaining ideas, be sure
to read tips for calorie-abiding substitutes.

≪o≫

The chapters are divided according to the
overriding theme of the recipes, but some of the recipes can easily
apply to more than one category. For example, something made on the
stovetop may not be in the section "On the Griddle," but in
"French Toast with Creative Breads."

≪o≫

Butter amounts for sautéing breads are subjective.
Amounts given are meant as guides. Use more or less according
to your personal preference, but be sure you have enough of a
lubricant to fully brown the toast.

On the Griddle

Baking Biscuit French Toast with Spiced Butter and Gingered Whipped Cream

⋖∽⋗

Like magic, this recipe puffs up a bit more than most French toasts. Start early in the day with preparation of the gingered cream (the cream is optional) and the spiced butter. Our testers found that men seemed particularly excited about this bread.

Have a French Toast smorgasbord when serving a brunch for friends. Cook up a variety of recipes, one from each section of this book, and set them out on a sideboard. The oven-baked and many of the special-occasion dishes can be done ahead of time.

PICTURE FACING CHAPTER OPENER: VICTORIAN TREASURE INN'S CINNAMON PECAN POCKETS, RECIPE ON PAGE 11

Gingered cream

1	8-ounce container whipping cream
5 to 6	pieces crystallized ginger

Spiced butter

$1/2$	cup (1 stick) butter, softened
$1/4$	teaspoon cinnamon
$1/4$	cup loosely packed brown sugar
$1/4$	teaspoon allspice
$1/8$	teaspoon nutmeg

Toast

6	eggs
$1/2$	cup biscuit mix
2	tablespoons sugar
$1/2$	teaspoon cinnamon
$1/2$	teaspoon nutmeg
$1^1/2$	cups milk
1	loaf French bread, heels removed
	Canola or safflower oil for frying

MAKES 6 TO 8 SERVINGS

Whip the cream until stiff, but not buttery. Finely dice the ginger and gently fold into the whipped cream. Cover and refrigerate for at least 6 hours.

To make the spiced butter, combine the butter, cinnamon, brown sugar, all-spice, and nutmeg in a small mixing bowl. Beat until fluffy.

When ready to serve, prepare the batter. In a medium bowl, beat the eggs until smooth. Blend in the biscuit mix, sugar, cinnamon, nutmeg, and milk. Mix until smooth.

Cut the bread into 1-inch-thick slices and dip in the batter until covered, but not soaked through. Heat approximately $1/2$-inch of cooking oil in a large skillet. When the oil is hot, place the bread slices in the pan and cook until golden brown on both sides. Serve with the spiced butter and the gingered cream.

—MEADOWLARK MANOR

[*3*]

Lemony French Toast Pouches with Yogurt Topping

I have made this recipe very often and it never fails to wake up the palate with its slightly tart flavor. It reminds me of tasting a lemon-meringue pie but without the calories.

Most grilled French toast recipes that call for sliced sandwich bread can be given an added touch by preparing them in the waffle iron instead of on the griddle. As long as the bread fits, the results will be a country-check pattern and a place for the syrup to collect in juicy pools.

Filling

	8 ounces cream cheese, softened
1/3	cup sugar
1	tablespoon lemon juice

Toast

1	loaf French bread, sliced crosswise into 1 to 1 1/2-inch thick slices, heels removed
2	tablespoons butter for sautéing

Batter

4	eggs
1/2	cup low-fat milk
1/2	teaspoon nutmeg
1	teaspoon grated lemon peel
1	teaspoon vanilla extract

Topping

Powdered sugar
Lemon yogurt

MAKES 4 TO 6 SERVINGS

*P*repare the filling by blending together the cream cheese, sugar, and lemon juice until creamy. Slice a pocket crosswise into the underside of each piece of bread. Spread

2 to 3 tablespoons of the cream cheese mixture into each pocket. Press the seam gently to close. For the batter, beat together the eggs, milk, nutmeg, lemon peel, and vanilla extract in a large bowl. Dip each stuffed bread pocket into the batter, coating both sides. Melt 2 tablespoons of butter in a large skillet. Cook the bread slices over moderate heat—about 2 minutes per side—or until browned.
Transfer each slice, on its side, to a serving plate. Lightly sift powdered sugar overtop. Place 1 rounded teaspoon of yogurt on top of each slice.

—PRESCOTT PINES INN

Grand Marnier Marinated French Toast

ᔕᗝᔕ

This French toast has great depth and perfectly complements the historic traditions of the Bailiwick inn, located across the street from where George Washington's last will is housed. It is delicious with breakfast sausage or, more appropriately, Virginia ham. Our testers felt that this was the best Grand Marnier French toast they ever had.

Neufchâtel cheese may be substituted for cream cheese to lighten calories. Add fruit to maple syrup such as mangoes. Purée 2 cups of peeled mangoes with 1/3 cup of maple syrup. Great on plain French toast.

6	eggs	8	3/4-inch-thick slices French bread
1	cup orange juice		Butter for sautéing
1/3	cup milk	3	tablespoons powdered sugar
1/4	cup sugar		Orange slices for garnish
1/4	teaspoon vanilla extract		
1/4	teaspoon salt		
2	tablespoons Grand Marnier		
	Grated peel of 1 orange		

MAKES 6 TO 8 SERVINGS

*P*repare the batter. Beat the eggs in a large bowl. Add the orange juice, milk, sugar, vanilla, salt, Grand Marnier, and orange rind. Mix well until all ingredients are combined. Dip the bread slices into the batter and arrange them on a baking sheet in a single layer. Pour any remaining batter over the top. Cover and refrigerate for 8 hours, turning occasionally. Bring the bread to room temperature before cooking.

Melt the butter in a large skillet set over medium heat. Add the bread slices and cook until browned on both sides. To serve, arrange the French toast on a platter and sprinkle with powdered sugar. Garnish with orange slices and drizzle with maple syrup.

—THE BAILIWICK INN

*R*ound Bread Toast Fruit Tart

⋘∘⋙

If you cannot find round bread at the market or bakery, use a heavy sliced bread and cut a round from each slice, using a large biscuit cutter, or make a circular cardboard or paper template and cut into the bread with kitchen scissors.

Get a large, heart cookie cutter (or make one) and cut bread out in this romantic shape. Prepare a grilled French toast recipe for special heartfelt occasions.

Tart

2	ripe pears, skinned and cut into ½-inch slices
2	oranges, peeled and cut into sections
1	cup red wine

Batter

4	eggs, beaten
1	cup milk
1	teaspoon vanilla extract
8	slices round bread

Assembly

Powdered sugar

MAKES 8 SERVINGS

Poach the pear and orange slices over high heat in the red wine for just a few minutes, or until the wine is reduced by half. (Fruit should still be rather firm.) Remove from the heat but keep warm.

Whisk together the eggs and the milk. Add the vanilla. Heat a nonstick griddle and dip the bread into the batter, coating both sides. Cook the bread over medium heat, flipping it to cook both sides to a golden brown. Center the cooked bread on the plate and fan the fruit around the top of the bread, alternating orange and pear slices. Sprinkle with powdered sugar.

—GAIL'S KITCHEN

Cinnamon Pecan Pockets with Chunky Spiced-Apple-Cider Sauce

~∞~

Even the innkeeper dresses up in Victorian finery at this splendid example of nine-teenth-century living in the twentieth century. Sometimes berries are added to the cream-cheese-and-nut filling, and complementary sauces are prepared, according to the season, such as cranberry-raspberry, blueberry-peach, and strawberry-rhubarb. No matter what the season, you will love the way your house smells when you make this French toast.

To lighten the calorie and cholesterol load, consider using egg substitutes.

Cinnamon Pecan Pockets (continued)

Sauce		*Toast*	
4	pounds red apples such as McIntosh apples, peeled, cored, and chopped in a small- to-medium dice	1	large loaf French bread
		8	ounces cream cheese, softened
		1/4	cup coarsely chopped pecans
2	tablespoons dark molasses	1	tablespoon vanilla extract
1 1/2	cups sugar	4	eggs
1	tablespoon cinnamon	1/4	cup milk
1	teaspoon nutmeg	1	teaspoon cinnamon
2	cups apple cider	1	teaspoon sugar
1	tablespoon vanilla extract	1/4	teaspoon salt
		2	tablespoons butter

MAKES 8 SERVINGS

*P*reheat the oven to 350°. In a 10x15-inch roasting pan, toss the apples with all of the remaining sauce ingredients. Bake for 1 hour, or until the apples are broken down and golden. (This sauce may be made ahead of time and refrigerated.) Otherwise, keep warm.

Cut the bread into 8 diagonal 1 1/2-inch slices, heels removed. Create a pocket from the crust to beyond the center of the bread. (Do not cut to the bottom.)

Mix together the cream cheese, nuts, and vanilla. Fill each bread pocket with 2 tablespoons of the mixture; set aside.

In a small bowl, beat together the eggs, milk, cinnamon, sugar, and salt. Heat the griddle and melt the butter. Bathe each pocket in the batter and sauté on the griddle, a few minutes on both sides, until golden brown.

Remove the bread from the griddle. Slice again diagonally, placing one half slice on a plate, overlapping the second half on top. Ladle the apple-cider sauce overtop and serve immediately. (Note: save any extra sauce for another recipe.)

—VICTORIAN TREASURE B&B

LEFT: VICTORIAN TREASURE B&B, LODI, WISCONSIN

Berry Low-Fat Yogurt French Toast

∽o∾

Who would have thought that it would ever come down to making French toast with yogurt not as a garnish or topping, but as part of the egg bath? But here it is—a nice choice for those times when you feel like being good. This little inn, in the picturesque harbor town of Camden, Maine, is painted cream and blue with cheerful mementos all about the house. No wonder this blueberry breakfast dish is so sought after.

LEFT: THE LOW-FAT BLUEBERRY FRENCH TOAST ON THE PORCH OF BLUE HARBOR HOUSE IN CAMDEN, MAINE

Berry Low-Fat Yogurt French Toast (continued)

Stuffing

6	ounces Neufchâtel cheese
6	ounces fat-free yogurt
3	ounces fat-free sour cream
1	cup fresh blueberries, crushed
1/2	cup frozen raspberries, crushed

Batter

2	8-ounce cartons Egg Beaters brand egg substitute
1	cup skim milk
1	teaspoon vanilla extract

Assembly

12	slices whole-wheat bread, crusts removed
	Powdered sugar
	Maple syrup

MAKES 4 SERVINGS

*B*egin by preparing the stuffing. Combine the cheese, yogurt, and sour cream in a large bowl.

Coat 6 slices of the bread with the creamy mixture and place—stuffing side up—in a 9x13-inch baking pan. Spoon blueberries and raspberries generously over the mixture. Spread more stuffing on the remaining 6 slices of bread, then place over the fruit to top off the sandwiches.

In a separate bowl, mix together the Egg Beaters, skim milk, and vanilla. Pour the batter over the sandwiches and soak for 30 minutes.

Sauté the sandwiches on a grill over medium heat until golden brown, turning several times. Slice the stuffed French toasts diagonally, and arrange on a large plate. Serve hot with a dusting of powdered sugar and warm maple syrup.

—BLUE HARBOR HOUSE

Hot Apple Pie French Toast

Tart apples, cut into small cubes, swathed in cinnamon and lemon juice, and then cooked between slices of thick egg-dipped bread, provide the kind of recipe French Manor breakfast cook Judy Raymond knows will satisfy her inn guests' discriminating tastes. This has quickly become one of my favorite French toasts, to which I sometimes add another bit of the old-time mixture of apple pie and cheddar. I place a slice of cheddar cheese into the bread pocket before filling with the apple stuffing.

LEFT: A MOUNTAIN VIEW FROM THE BREAKFAST PATIO OF THE FRENCH MANOR

4	Granny Smith apples
1	teaspoon cinnamon
2	tablespoons all-purpose flour
1	teaspoon lemon juice
3/4	cup sugar
4	eggs
2	cups milk or half-and-half
1/2	teaspoon nutmeg
1	tablespoon vanilla extract
6	(1-inch-thick) slices hearty day-old bread
	Powdered sugar

MAKES 6 SERNINGS

Cut the apples into 1/4-inch cubes. Place them in a pan with enough water to cover. Cook the apples over high heat, removing them from the heat when the water reaches a boil. Drain the apples and gently toss them together with the cinnamon, flour, lemon juice, and 1/4 cup of the sugar. Set aside.

In a large bowl beat the eggs. Add the milk or half-and-half, the remaining 1/2 cup of sugar, the nutmeg, and the vanilla.

Make a pocket in each bread slice by inserting the knife into one end of the bread. Cut from side to side (crust to crust) without cutting through. Open the slice and fill generously with the apple-pie filling. Cook on a hot, greased griddle over medium heat (cook slowly) until golden brown. Sprinkle with powdered sugar and serve with maple syrup (if desired) and any extra apple filling.

— THE FRENCH MANOR

LEFT: THE FRENCH MANOR, SOUTH STERLING, PENNSYLVANIA

Baked in the Oven

Victorian-Baked Caramel French Toast

Rich yet light and lacy, just like a Victorian dress, this toast highly complements the old-fashioned dining room at the inn, which is adorned in nineteenth-century finery. It will grace your table with the same buoyant mood, and wow, is this delicious! You can make this recipe a day ahead of serving time. Staying at this inn will remind you of visiting a little European village.

1	cup packed brown sugar
1/3	cup butter
2	tablespoons light corn syrup
6	1-inch-thick slices French bread
5	eggs
1 1/2	cups milk
1	teaspoon cinnamon
	Strawberries, peaches, or pears, thinly sliced, or fresh blueberries or raspberries
	Powdered sugar for garnish

MAKES 6 SERVINGS

In a small saucepan, combine the brown sugar, butter, and corn syrup. Stirring constantly, cook over moderate heat just until the butter melts. Pour the brown sugar mixture into an ungreased 9x13-inch baking dish. Arrange the bread slices in a single layer overtop the brown sugar mixture; set aside.

To prepare the batter, beat the eggs, milk, and cinnamon in a medium mixing bowl until combined. Pour the batter over the French bread in the pan, saturating all the slices. Cover and refrigerate for 2 hours or prepare the day before.

Preheat the oven to 350°. Uncover the baking dish and cook the French toast for 30 to 35 minutes, or until the center appears set and the top is lightly browned. Let stand about 10 minutes before serving. Top with fresh fruit and powdered sugar.

—CORNER GEORGE INN

Baked Blueberry French Bread

∽∾∽

I like this blueberry recipe because there is a substantial presence of blueberries, giving the French toast a whole new face. A nice substitute is to use fresh blueberries, the kind you go out and pick that are very plump and juicy. When the berries are really sweet, I even cut down on the sugar in this recipe. Begin this recipe a few hours ahead of time.

A few drops of vanilla extract and a teaspoon or so of powdered sugar will further enrich any batter.

1	loaf Italian bread	1/2	cup sugar
4	eggs	1	teaspoon cinnamon
1/2	cup milk	1	teaspoon cornstarch
1/4	teaspoon baking powder	2	tablespoons butter, melted
1	teaspoon vanilla extract	1/4	cup powdered sugar
21/2	cups fresh or frozen blueberries		

MAKES 8 SERVINGS

Slice the bread on the diagonal to create eight 3/4-inch-thick pieces, heels removed. Arrange the bread slices in a 10x15-inch baking dish.

To make the batter, whip together the eggs, milk, baking powder, and vanilla in a medium bowl. Slowly pour the mixture over the bread, turning each slice to coat completely. Cover the dish with plastic wrap and refrigerate for at least 1 hour, but preferably overnight.

Preheat the oven to 425°. Coat another 10x15-inch baking dish with cooking oil spray. Sprinkle the blueberries over the bottom of the pan. Mix together the sugar, cinnamon, and cornstarch and pour evenly overtop the berries. Tightly wedge the bread slices over the blueberries, wettest side up. Brush the bread with melted butter. Bake the French toast in the center of the oven for 20 to 25 minutes, or until golden brown.

To serve, place the toast—berry-side down—on warmed plates. Stir the remaining berry mixture in the baking dish, then scoop over the toast. Sprinkle with powdered sugar.

—SEVEN SISTERS INN

Cream Cheese French Toast Bake with Strawberry Sauce

∽∘∾

Simple and sweet, this trusty French toast comes from a stately Victorian manor house, tucked into the quiet hills of rural New Jersey, but within walking distance of an exciting little village. The inn also uses a potato bread and $2/3$ cream cheese with $1/3$ Ricotta for a slight change of pace with this very same recipe.

Generally speaking, skim milk may be substituted for whole milk in most French toast dipping batters.

Cream Cheese French Toast Bake (continued)

Toast			*Sauce*	
1	loaf firm sliced bread		2	cups fresh strawberries, sliced
1	8-ounce package cream cheese, softened		2	cups strawberry preserves
10	eggs			
1½	cups half-and-half			
¼	cup maple syrup			
¼	cup (½ stick) butter, melted			

MAKES 6 TO 8 SERVINGS

Cut the bread into 1½-inch cubes and layer half of the cubes into a 9x13-inch baking dish. Slice the cream cheese into small pieces and sprinkle evenly over the bread cubes. Sprinkle the remaining bread cubes over the cream cheese layer.

In a mixing bowl, stir well the eggs, half-and-half, maple syrup, and melted butter. Pour the egg mixture evenly over the bread cubes, pressing the cubes down firmly to soak up the liquid. Cover and refrigerate overnight.

Preheat the oven to 350°. Bake the toast for 40 to 50 minutes.

While the toast bakes, prepare the strawberry sauce. In a medium saucepan, combine the strawberries and preserves. Stir over medium heat until the mixture is just warmed. Remove the toast from the oven and serve with the warm sauce.

—THE WOOLVERTON INN

LEFT: AN ELEGANT HALLWAY AT THE WOOLVERTON INN IN STOCKTON, NEW JERSEY

Macadamia-Banana French Toast

✼

Nice and fruity and full of fiber, this rendition of French toast is a bit offbeat, but the flavors and ingredients balance well together. You will never fail to pleasantly surprise someone with this dish, and it makes great use of overripe bananas.

2	bananas, ripe or unripe
4	eggs
1	cup milk
1	3½-ounce jar macadamia nuts, finely chopped
1	teaspoon vanilla extract
½	teaspoon cinnamon or allspice
8 to 10	slices whole-wheat bread

MAKES 4 SERVINGS

*P*reheat the oven to 475° and lightly grease or spray 2 nonstick baking sheets. In a blender or food processor, blend together 1 of the bananas, the eggs, milk, half of the nuts, the vanilla, and the cinnamon until well combined. Pour the mixture into a large shallow dish and dip the bread slices into the liquid until well absorbed on both sides. Arrange the bread on the prepared baking sheets. Bake for 8 to 10 minutes (keep checking every 5 minutes to be sure the toast is not burning) or until golden.

When done, remove the toast from the baking sheets and slice each piece diagonally. Slice the remaining banana and arrange overtop the toast. Sprinkle with chopped macadamia nuts.

—HOWARD CREEK RANCH

French toast could always use some color and another texture. Festoon this morning meal with cheerful edible flowers.

Apple-and-Cinnamon Toast Cobbler

✧◦✧

If you want to have some fun with this recipe, serve it with a small dollop of vanilla ice cream. Yes, in the morning! What a way to ensure you will smile throughout the day.

Cut grilled French toasts into rounds as appetizers for brunches. Top the rounds with strawberry halves and powdered sugar or make up any combination of fruits or preserves, nuts or other garnishes.

1	6-ounce French bread baguette, heels removed		2	large tart apples, peeled, cored, and thinly sliced
4	eggs		1/2	cup brown sugar
1	cup milk		1	teaspoon cinnamon
1/4	teaspoon baking powder		2	tablespoons butter, melted
1	teaspoon vanilla extract			

MAKES 8 SERVINGS

Cut the baguette into 1-inch slices and arrange slices in a 9x13-inch baking dish. In a mixing bowl, whisk together the eggs, milk, baking powder, and vanilla. Pour the egg mixture over the French bread slices, turning each to coat completely. Cover

the dish with plastic wrap and let stand until all of the liquid is absorbed, about 15 to 20 minutes.

Preheat the oven to 450°. Lightly grease another 9x13-inch baking dish (nonstick preferred). Place the sliced apples in a layer along the bottom of the pan. Sprinkle brown sugar and cinnamon over the apples. Arrange the soaked bread slices overtop and brush with melted butter. Bake for 25 minutes, or until golden brown. Serve with warm maple syrup and maybe some of that ice cream.

—NORTH GARDEN INN

A VIEW ACROSS THE COURTYARD AT BECKMANN INN

Cranberry French Toast Bake

∽∾

Dried cranberries bake into a cinnamon egg batter, offering up a browned fruit bread. Make this recipe the night before and serve it with fresh fruit and breakfast sausage. This is particularly nice around holidays, but the toast will prove festive anytime it is served.

BECKMANN INN, SAN ANTONIO

Syrup and sauces are not always a must for French toast. Consider grilled toast with slices of fresh fruit—the juicier the better.

Cranberry French Toast Bake (continued)

6	eggs
2/3	cup sugar
1	tablespoon cinnamon
3	cups milk
1	pound French bread, cut into 1/2-inch slices
1/4 to 1/2	cup lightly packed brown sugar
3/4	tablespoons dried cranberries

MAKES 6 TO 8 SERVINGS

*W*hisk together the eggs with the sugar and cinnamon until well blended. Whisk in the milk just until incorporated.

Coat a 9x13-inch pan with cooking oil spray. Place the bread on the bottom of the pan, filling in any holes with more bread. Pour the egg-and-cinnamon mixture evenly over the bread.

Mix together the brown sugar and cranberries, adding more brown sugar to taste. Sprinkle evenly on top of the bread mixture. Refrigerate overnight.

Next morning, preheat the oven to 325°. Bake the French toast for 50 to 60 minutes or until a rich brown. Serve immediately.

—BECKMANN INN

French Toast with Creative Breads

Sourdough French Toast with Honey Orange Glaze

√

The provocative flavor of the sourdough offers a nice contrast to the sweet glaze. I like using the bacon rendering for sautéing the toast, or you can use the rendering of any breakfast meat you have sautéed to go along with the French toast.

Glaze		Toast	
1	cup water	1	egg
2	cups sugar	1/3	cup orange juice
	Grated peel of 1 medium orange	6	slices sourdough bread
	Juice from 1 medium orange		Bacon fat or 1 tablespoon butter
1/4	cup (1/2 stick) butter		Orange slices for garnish
1	cup honey		

MAKES 2 SERVINGS

Make the glaze first. Combine the water, sugar, orange zest, and orange juice in a saucepan. Stir over high heat until the mixture begins to boil. Then, lower the heat and simmer for 10 minutes, stirring occasionally. Add the butter and honey. Stir until the butter is melted. Keep warm. (Tip: The glaze will keep several weeks in the refrigerator, so you may make it in advance).

Prepare the French toast batter by mixing together the egg and orange juice. Pour the liquid into a small baking pan. Dip the bread slices into the egg mixture, coating evenly on both sides. Melt the butter in a preheated skillet. Sauté the bread a few minutes on each side or until golden brown. Serve warm, drizzled with the honey glaze. Garnish with the orange slices.

—DOANLEIGH WALLAGH INN

PICTURE FACING CHAPTER OPENER: A PAINTING OF THE SETTLERS INN, AND THE INN'S ARTISTIC BREADS

ANOTHER VIEW OF THE FRENCH MANOR, THIS TIME THE VERSAILLES ROOM

Panettone French Toast with Cinnamon Raisin Sauce

◈

Legend has it that panettone bread, which originated in Italy, was so named by the townsfolk when they heard that a poor baker supplied bread as his daughter's dowry to a rich nobleman. The baker's name was Tony. *Pane* in Italian means bread, hence the name panettone (pah-na-tony). How romantic. This yeast bread with citron and raisins is now available in specialty stores all year round. I often substitute crushed granola for the cornflake topping. The Gingerbread Mansion is one of the most photographed inns in America, and I have been one of those shutterbugs, who like to capture it from every beautiful angle.

If you are making your own bread for French toast, remember that New Englanders believe that you must knead the bread from forty-five minutes to one hour straight. Any pause in the process will injure the bread.

Panettone French Toast (continued)

Sauce		Toast	
2	tablespoons butter	6	eggs
1	tablespoon all-purpose flour	1¹/₂	cups half-and-half
1	cup water	³/₄	cup light cream or milk
1	cup sugar	¹/₂	cup sugar
1	teaspoon vanilla extract	¹/₄	cup dark rum
1	teaspoon cinnamon	1¹/₂	teaspoons grated orange peel
¹/₂	cup raisins	3	teaspoons vanilla extract
		¹/₄	teaspoon cinnamon
		¹/₄	teaspoon ground nutmeg
			Butter for sautéing
		8	(1 to 1 ¹/₂-inch) slices day-old panettone
		2	cups cornflakes, crushed and set out on a flat plate
			Powdered sugar for garnish

MAKES 8 SERVINGS

*T*o make the sauce, melt the butter in a saucepan over medium heat. Blend in the flour, stirring constantly for 1 to 2 minutes, until the mixture bubbles, forming a roux. Remove the pan from the heat and gradually whisk in the water, then the sugar. Return to the heat and cook until thick and just beginning to boil. Add the vanilla, cinnamon, and raisins, mixing well. Keep warm.

Prepare the toast. In a large bowl, beat the eggs slightly. Add the creams, sugar, rum, orange peel, vanilla, cinnamon, and nutmeg, beating well. Melt a tablespoon or so of butter in a medium-hot skillet. Dip the bread slices in the egg mixture, then in the crushed cereal, turning to coat both sides. Sauté the bread slices a few minutes on each side or until golden brown. When done, remove to a serving platter, sprinkle with powdered sugar, and serve with the sauce.

—GINGERBREAD MANSION INN

LEFT: THE GINGERBREAD MANSION, FERNDALE, CALIFORNIA

Brandied Challah French Toast with Apples, Pecans, and Caramel Sauce

Thin walls of golden-brown egg crust shield a light airy texture, making up the traditional Jewish yeast bread, challah. Here, we spread a nutty apple cream cheese over the bread before cooking. Challah is tasty and soft but absorbent, showing us a sensual side to French toast.

Cream Cheese Spread

4	ounces cream cheese
1	medium Granny Smith or other tart apple, peeled, quartered, and cored
1/4	cup finely chopped pecans
1/4	cup granulated light brown sugar

Toast

4	eggs
1 1/2	cups half-and-half cream
2	tablespoons brandy
1/2	teaspoon nutmeg
1/2	teaspoon cinnamon

1/2	teaspoon mace
8	(3/4-inch thick) slices challah bread, heels removed

Caramel Sauce

3/4	cup sugar
1/4	cup lemon juice
1/2	cup heavy cream

Assembly

2	tablespoons or so butter
1	medium tart apple, peeled, quartered, and cored
1/2	cup finely chopped pecans

MAKES 4 SERVINGS

In a food processor, smooth together the cream cheese, apples, the 1/4 cup pecans, and brown sugar. Cover and refrigerate.

Preheat the oven to 350°. In a medium bowl, combine the eggs, cream, brandy, nutmeg, cinnamon and mace. Soak the bread in the egg mixture, turning to coat both sides. Set aside.

Meanwhile, make the caramel sauce. In a small saucepan over medium-low heat, cook the sugar and the lemon juice until the mixture turns golden. Reduce the heat to low and gradually whisk in the heavy cream. Keep the sauce warm.

In a large skillet begin to cook the challah. Melt the butter. Add the bread slices and cook until golden brown on both sides. Transfer the French toast to a baking sheet and cut the slices in half diagonally. Divide the cream cheese spread evenly among the slices. Bake 5 to 10 minutes or until the cheese is warm.

Meanwhile, thinly slice the remaining apple quarters. In the same skillet, melt the butter and sauté the apple slices until tender.

To serve, drizzle the caramel sauce onto individual serving plates. Divide the French toast, placing pieces diagonally on each plate. Top with the sautéed apple slices. Sprinkle pecans overtop.

—GAIL'S KITCHEN

Cinnamon-Swirl Bread French Toast

❧

They love cinnamon at Canyon Villa. The spice is the same rust color as the age-old buttes or red rocks that appear in every villa window. You can find cinnamon-swirl bread in most supermarkets.

Just by changing the dipping batter, you can invent a new French toast. Consider different fresh juices to add with the eggs. Add chocolate milk instead of regular milk. Give it a java jolt by adding in a few tablespoons of concentrated coffee. Perhaps it is mint you enjoy. Add a few drops of crème de menthe liqueur. The possibilities are limitless. Experiment and use your imagination.

8	eggs
1	cup milk
2	teaspoons vanilla extract
16	(1-inch thick) slices cinnamon swirl bread
	Orange slices for garnish

*B*eat the eggs in a large bowl. Pour in the milk and vanilla, beating until the mixture is smooth. Soak the bread slices into the batter, coating both sides.

Heat a griddle. Cook the cinnamon swirl toast for a few minutes on each side or until golden brown. Serve with maple syrup and garnish with orange slices.

—CANYON VILLA

Pound Cake French Toast

∽◦∾

Some of the better store-bought pound cakes will do well in this recipe, which also makes a splendid dessert.

MEMORIES OF THE GENEVIEVE ROOM AT THE FRENCH MANOR MAKE ME EAGER FOR MY NEXT VISIT TO AN INN.

Have several pitchers out on the table for syrup. Some people like to keep pouring that golden nectar on after every few bites. That way, no one will be embarrassed to ask, Please pass the syrup. I have a collection of individual serving-size pitchers and like to put one at each place setting.

1	egg, beaten
1	teaspoon orange extract
1/4	cup whole or skim milk
1	teaspoon sugar
1/2	teaspoon cinnamon
2	(1-inch) slices plain pound cake
	Canola oil for sautéing

MAKES 2 SERVINGS

In a mixing bowl, beat together the egg, extract, milk, sugar, and cinnamon. Dip the pound cake slices into the batter, coating both sides.

Place the slices on an oiled griddle over medium heat. Cook the cake for 2 to 3 minutes (flipping carefully) on each side, or until golden brown. Serve immediately with your favorite syrup and fresh fruit.

—GAIL'S KITCHEN

Orange-and-Macadamia Sally Lunn Bread French Toast

❧

Sally Lunn is a historic, non-yeast bread, popular around the time of Thomas Jefferson. Jefferson's daughter, Martha, owned the house and property that now houses Clifton, a country inn filled with history and wonderful things to eat. The orange bread crossed with the nutty macadamias would have tickled Mr. Jefferson's eclectic palate. This recipe makes 2 loaves, so you will have extra, but it freezes well for your next French toast morning, or serve it with butter and jelly or by itself.

CLIFTON COUNTRY INN

Bread			2	cups chopped macadamia nuts, plus more for garnish
4	eggs (at room temperature), separated		2	tablespoons butter for sautéing
1	cup sugar			
3	tablespoons all-purpose flour		Sauce	
2	tablespoons baking powder		1	cup fresh-squeezed orange juice, strained
1/8	teaspoon salt			
1	cup milk		1/2	cup sugar
1/2	cup orange juice		Batter	
1	teaspoon orange extract		3	eggs
	Grated peel from 3 oranges		1	cup half-and-half
1/4	cup (1/2 stick) butter, melted		1/4	cup sugar

MAKES 4 SERVINGS

*P*reheat the oven to 350°. Whip the egg whites until stiff peaks form. Set aside.

In a large bowl, cream together the egg yolks and the sugar. In another bowl, mix together the flour, baking powder, and salt. Mix together the milk, orange juice, orange extract, and the orange zest. Alternately pour the dry mixture and the wet mixture into the egg-and-sugar mixture. Add the butter and stir in the nuts. Fold in the stiffened egg whites. Pour into two 9x5-inch nonstick loaf pans and bake 30 to 40 minutes or until golden brown. Let cool.

Meanwhile prepare the sauce by bringing the orange juice and sugar to a boil. Turn down to a simmer and cook another few minutes or until the mixture is no longer cloudy. Keep warm. When the bread is baked and cooled, blend all of the batter ingredients, mixing well.

Slice the Sally Lunn bread into 1-inch-thick pieces. Soak the bread in the batter and cook on a hot buttered griddle for a few minutes on each side until golden brown. Pool 2 ounces of sauce on the plate. Top with 2 slices of toast. Garnish with the extra nuts and add kiwi and bananas or any other combination of tropical fruit.

—CLIFTON COUNTRY INN

Croissant French Toast Sandwiches

⌘

Cream cheese and apricot jam are the stuffings for this dish, but the inn also substitutes with ham and Swiss cheese, totally altering its personality. Leave out the vanilla if making the latter. This inn overlooks tall piney forests, scenic farmland, and sparkling waters of Puget Sound.

Most recipes for the griddle may be sautéed in a pan coated with nonstick cooking spray. Or, if you use a nonstick griddle or pan, you can get away with less butter.

Toast

1	teaspoon milk
8	ounces cream cheese, softened
6	croissants, split lengthwise
	Apricot jam

Batter

3/4	cup half-and-half (or milk)
3	eggs
1/4	cup biscuit mix
1	teaspoon vanilla extract

Assembly

Oil for cooking
Fresh berries of choice
Yogurt for garnish

MAKES 6 SERVINGS

*S*tir the milk into the cream cheese, adding more if necessary to make it smooth. Spread half of the croissants with the cream cheese. Cover the cheese with a light layer of jam as desired. Cover with the top half of the croissant.

In a blender, mix together the half-and-half, eggs, biscuit mix, and vanilla. Soak the sandwiches in the batter until well saturated (about 30 seconds).

Fill a large skillet with 1/4-inch oil. Heat the oil over medium heat and cook the croissants, until browned and puffy on each side. Drain on a paper towel. Garnish with fresh berries or yogurt.

—TURTLEBACK FARM

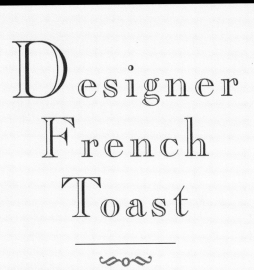

Designer French Toast

Cardamom French Toast with Red Currant Syrup

The inviting, spicy-sweet flavor of the cardamom is a brilliant addition to the world of French toasts. I highly suggest not substituting anything else for the red currant jelly. Red currants are so sweet and delicious that you can eat them right off the bush. When I had this at the inn, I also enjoyed an incredible vista of mountains and water. The Lodge on Lake Lure is a best-kept secret!

If an egg floats in cool salted water, it is not fresh. Fresh eggs will sink to the bottom of the bowl.

PICTURE FACING CHAPTER OPENER: A BEAUTIFUL MOUNTAIN LAKE ONLY ENHANCES THE TASTE OF THE CARDAMON FRENCH TOAST.

Toast		Syrup	
1 1/2	cups milk	1	cup red currant jelly
2	eggs	1/2	cup orange juice
3	tablespoons sugar	3/4	teaspoon cardamom
2	teaspoons grated orange peel	3	tablespoons butter
1/2	teaspoon vanilla extract		
1/2	teaspoon salt		
1/2	teaspoon cardamom		
12	(3/4-inch thick) slices French bread		
1/2	cup (1 stick) butter		

MAKES 4 SERVINGS

*M*ix together the milk, eggs, sugar, orange peel, vanilla, salt, and cardamom. Place the bread slices in a baking dish and pour the egg mixture overtop. Cover and refrigerate overnight.

Melt the butter in a large skillet over low heat. Drain the bread and place the slices in the skillet. Cook slowly—about 5 minutes—on each side until golden brown.

Prepare the red currant syrup. In a saucepan, heat the jelly with the orange juice and cardamom, stirring occasionally until the jelly melts. Bring the mixture to a boil and cook until a syrup begins to form—about 3 minutes. Remove the syrup from the heat and whip in the butter with a wire whisk until melted and fully incorporated. Serve over the French toast.

—THE LODGE ON LAKE LURE

Sour Cream French Toast with Pineapple and Coconut

∽o∾

A taste of Hawaii comes through in this tropical version of a grilled French toast that is crisp but moist enough that you can do without a syrup topping.

4	eggs		1/4	cup milk
1	teaspoon vanilla extract		8	slices day-old bread, crusts removed
1	tablespoon maple syrup		2	tablespoons butter
1	tablespoon sour cream			Powdered sugar for garnish
1	tablespoon sugar			Shredded coconut for garnish
1	8-ounce can crushed pineapple, drained			

MAKES 4 SERVINGS

In a large bowl, combine the eggs, vanilla, syrup, sour cream, sugar, pineapple, and milk. Blend until smooth. Cut the bread slices in half on the diagonal and arrange them in a large shallow dish. Pour the egg-pineapple mixture over the bread, then turn to coat the other side.

In a large, nonstick skillet, melt some of the butter over medium heat. Place a few pieces of the soaked bread in the pan and cook until just browned on the bottom. Turn and brown the reverse side. Use the remaining butter as needed.

To serve, dust the French toast slices with powdered sugar and sprinkle with shredded coconut.

—MY BLUE HEAVEN B&B

Unless otherwise stated, most recipes calling for French bread mean a large loaf of the wider bread, not a thin baguette. Those calling for Italian bread mean the crusty long loaves.

Raisin-Bread French Toast Sandwiches with Orange Sauce

❧

The inn where this recipe hails from is a simply charming B&B in the midst of high Victorians. Manor House is a favorite of mine with its antiques and casual manner. I love the room on the third level with the old brick walls.

Sauce		Toast	
1	6-ounce container orange juice concentrate	12	slices raisin bread
1/2	cup (1 stick) butter	6	ounces cream cheese
1/2	cup sugar	4	eggs
		3	tablespoons sugar
		3	tablespoons citrus liqueur or orange extract
		2	tablespoons butter

MAKES 6 SERVINGS

Prepare the orange sauce. Combine the orange juice concentrate, butter, and sugar in a small saucepan. Simmer over medium-low heat until well blended. Keep warm.

Spread 6 slices of the raisin bread evenly with cream cheese. Top each with a second slice of bread to form sandwiches.

To make the batter, whisk together the eggs, sugar, and liqueur. Dip the sandwiches in the egg mixture, turning to coat both sides.

Melt the butter on a hot griddle. Sauté the sandwiches a few minutes on each side or until golden brown.

—MANOR HOUSE INN

Part of the charm of traveling to B&Bs on back roads is coming across quiet country churches like this one in New England.

For another syrup substitute, purée fresh or frozen raspberries in a blender, adding a little sugar if necessary.

Brandied Cranberry-Ricotta French Toast with Cinnamon Orange Syrup

✧

Garam masala is an Indian ingredient made up of a combination of warm and soothing spices. It is widely available in specialty stores or substitute with a mixture of ground cloves, cinnamon, cardamom, and coriander. You must have this decadent French toast at least once in your life. The many intriguing facets of this recipe remind me of the modern stained-glass work on Shelburne Inn windows.

Cinnamon-Orange Syrup

1 1/2	cups water
2	cups sugar
3	cups (12 ounces) fresh cranberries
1/2	cup dry white wine
	Juice and grated peel of 1 orange
1	cinnamon stick

Filling

2	tablespoons butter
1/2	cup fresh cranberries, chopped
1/2	cup walnuts, chopped
3	tablespoons brandy
1	teaspoon garam masala
2	tablespoons honey
2	cups Ricotta cheese

Toast

1	loaf French bread, cut into 6 (2-inch) slices, heels removed
6	eggs, beaten
1/2	cup heavy cream
1/2	cup orange juice
1/4	teaspoon cinnamon
1	tablespoon grated orange peel
1	teaspoon or more Grand Marnier
1/8	teaspoon nutmeg

MAKES 6 SERVINGS

*P*repare the syrup. In a small saucepan bring the water and sugar to a boil. Add the cranberries, wine, orange juice, orange zest, and cinnamon stick, and bring the mixture to a boil. Reduce the heat and simmer for 15 minutes or until the cranberries are tender. Remove and reserve the cinnamon stick. Strain the mixture, reserving the liquid and placing the solids in a food processor. Process for 1 minute and transfer to a saucepan with the reserved liquid and cinnamon stick. Simmer for 15 minutes or until thickened. Discard the cinnamon stick. Keep the syrup warm.

To make the filling, melt the butter in a nonstick skillet and sauté 1/2 cup of cranberries and the nuts until the nuts brown. Add the brandy and flambe in the pan. Add the garam masala and honey. Stir in the Ricotta. Remove the pan from the heat and set the filling aside.

Make a cut in the center top of each piece of bread to create a pocket. Fill each pocket with the cheese mixture, then firmly press the pockets closed.

In a large bowl, mix together the eggs, cream, orange juice, cinnamon, orange rind, Grand Marnier, and nutmeg. Submerge each stuffed bread slice in the mixture for 20 to 30 seconds, until a good amount of the mixture is absorbed. Sauté the bread on a hot griddle, turning to cook each side until golden brown. Serve warm with cinnamon-orange syrup.

—THE SHELBURNE INN

Just for Fun

Butter-Almond Ice-Cream-Dipped French Toast

∽◦∾

I know, I know. Ice cream in the morning? But if you analyze this recipe, you realize that it really is not using such out-of-character ingredients. French toast is often dipped in heavy cream, so why not ice cream that has even more flavor?

Honey makes a nice simple topping for French toast. Coat the inside of a pitcher with vegetable oil and the honey will slip right back into the jar after serving.

PICTURE FACING CHAPTER OPENER: FRENCH TOAST SUNDAE, RECIPE ON PAGE 82

2	cups butter-almond or butter-pecan ice cream
5	eggs
3	tablespoons Amaretto liqueur
12	($^3/_4$-inch thick) slices French bread
	Sliced or slivered almonds
	Butter for sautéing
	Powdered sugar

MAKES 4 SERVINGS

Melt the ice cream at room temperature or in a microwave set on high for 2 to 3 minutes. Add the eggs and beat until blended. Beat in the Amaretto until thoroughly mixed. Dip the bread slices into the mixture, coating well and pressing the almonds from the ice cream into the bread.

Melt the butter in a large skillet. Cook the bread for a few minutes on both sides or until golden brown. To serve, slightly overlap 3 slices of French toast per plate and dust with powdered sugar. Garnish with almonds and serve with maple syrup.

—MAPLEWOOD INN

RIGHT: A DRAMATIC BEDROOM AT THE INN AT ROUND BARN FARM IN WAITSFIELD, VERMONT

Chocolate French-Bread Pockets with Pistachios

⚜

Breakfast at Chicago Pike Inn is always bountiful but elegant in a wood-trimmed dining room with soft pastel accents. From fruit soups to brandied fruits, outrageous muffins, and baked egg dishes, it is always an interesting morning. Even chocolate makes it to the breakfast table, as in this recipe.

Keep a kitchen journal and jot down happy thoughts and experiences you have had working in the kitchen and enjoying food.

Chocolate French-Bread Pockets (continued)

6	(1-inch thick) slices Italian bread	$^1/_8$	teaspoon cinnamon
1	3-ounce chunk semisweet chocolate	$^1/_8$	teaspoon nutmeg
6	teaspoons chopped unsalted pistachio nuts	4	tablespoons butter, divided
			Powdered sugar
			Orange slices for garnish
3	eggs		Chocolate curls or shavings for garnish
1	tablespoon orange liqueur, optional		
$^3/_4$	cup milk		
2	tablespoons sugar		
1	teaspoon vanilla extract		

MAKES 6 SERVINGS

*C*ut a pocket horizontally in each slice of bread through the top crust. Divide the chocolate bar evenly into 6 rectangles. Fill each bread slice with a piece of chocolate and 1 teaspoon of pistachios.

Prepare the batter by whisking together the eggs, liqueur, milk, sugar, vanilla, cinnamon, and nutmeg in a shallow dish. Dip the filled bread slices—one at a time—into the egg mixture, carefully turning to coat both sides.

In a large skillet, melt 1 tablespoon of the butter over medium heat. Cook the slices on the hot pan until golden brown on both sides, adding more butter as needed. Transfer the French toast to heated plates and dust with powdered sugar just before serving. Garnish with orange slices and chocolate curls or shavings, if desired.

—THE CHICAGO PIKE INN

LEFT: CHICAGO PIKE INN, COLDWATER, MICHIGAN

Eggnog-and-Raisin-Bread
French Toast Strips

ᢏᢛᣳ

You do not have to wait for the holidays to prepare this unusual French toast. If eggnog is not available, make your own. The nutty flavor imparted by the eggnog truly enriches this French toast. I add a little nutmeg to Ravenscroft's recipe. This style French toast can also be served as a side dish to a breakfast entrée, such as an egg dish.

12	(1-inch thick) slices raisin bread
2	cups eggnog
1/2	cup butter, melted
	Powdered sugar

MAKES 6 SERVINGS

*P*reheat the oven to 450°. Remove the crusts from the bread slices and cut the bread into 1-inch-wide strips. Pour the eggnog into a shallow pan and dip each bread strip in the eggnog, turning each piece to coat well. Lightly grease a 9x13-inch baking dish.

Bake the strips in the oven for 5 to 8 minutes or until golden brown. Remove the pan from the oven. Turn the toast strips and brush the reverse sides with the rest of the melted butter. Return the pan to the oven and continue baking for another 3 to 4 minutes or until golden brown. Sprinkle with powdered sugar just before serving with maple syrup, if desired.

—RAVENSCROFT INN

Warm your serving plates in the oven, since French toast generally cools down quickly.

Peanut-Butter-and-Jelly French Toast Sandwiches

❦

In my kitchen, there's a certain someone who likes just about everything with peanut butter on it, so this passionate tribute to his particular taste goes a long way. I suggest using Mom's idea of Arnolds Brick Oven Bread here because of its density. (To read more about this, see "Lost Breads," page xi.)

CANYON VILLA: A PLACE I THINK ABOUT WHEN MAKING JUST SUCH A "JUST-FOR-FUN" FRENCH TOAST.

Look through a stack of old magazines to recharge your heart and spirit. Look for new ideas and more delicious recipes to serve.

1/2	cup creamy peanut butter (crunchy will also do)
8	slices white bread
1	cup strawberry preserves, or of choice
4	eggs, lightly beaten
1/2	cup milk
2	tablespoons butter

MAKES 4 SERVINGS

Spread the peanut butter evenly over 4 bread slices. Spread the preserves evenly overtop. Cap with remaining bread slices to form a sandwich; set aside.

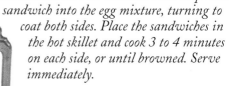

Combine the eggs and milk in a shallow dish. Melt the butter in a large nonstick skillet set over medium heat. Dip each sandwich into the egg mixture, turning to coat both sides. Place the sandwiches in the hot skillet and cook 3 to 4 minutes on each side, or until browned. Serve immediately.

—GAIL'S KITCHEN

French Toast Sundae

✥

At the Inn at the Round Barn Farm, they call this a Fruit-Drenched French Toast. But I can't help but rename it and I'm sure you will agree as you read the recipe. At holiday time, the inn makes this with eggnog instead of the milk and cream. Feel free to sprinkle nuts on top of your "sundae."

8	eggs	1	cup cornflakes, crushed
1½	cups milk		Assortment of fresh sliced fruits in season
½	cup heavy cream		Maple syrup
1	tablespoon vanilla extract		Powdered sugar
⅛	teaspoon freshly ground nutmeg		Whipped cream
12	slices Italian bread, sliced 1-inch thick		

MAKES 6 SERVINGS

*P*reheat griddle to 375°. In a large mixing bowl, whisk eggs, milk, and heavy cream until well combined, about 3 to 4 minutes. This allows the heavy cream almost to

whip creating a light batter. Add the vanilla. Pour mixture through a strainer to remove egg excess. Add the vanilla. Pour mixture through a strainer to remove egg excess. Add nutmeg. Dip bread into mixture but do not soak. Dip one side of the bread into cornflakes. Repeat with all slices.

Grease griddle and cook bread with the cornflakes side down first. Flip when golden brown. Place two slices on a plate and top with fruit and maple syrup. Dust with powdered sugar. Add a dollop of whipped cream, if desired.

—INN AT ROUND BARM FARM

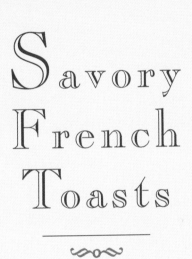

Savory
French
Toasts

Whole Grain French Toast Stuffed with Brie and Sundried Peaches

~~~

The Beaufort is my idea of a quintessential country inn—intimate dining, creative menu, old-fashioned hospitality, pampered rooms, and enchantment around every corner, just like this breakfast recipe created by Chef Peter DeJong. He also suggests serving it for lunch, accompanied by soup and a salad with raspberry dressing. Sundried peaches are available in specialty stores, but do not use regular dried peaches since they are too hard.

3	ounces Brie cheese, cut into $1/4$-inch slices
4	slices day-old, whole-grain bread
8	sundried peaches, cut into $1/8$-inch slices
2	eggs, beaten
1	tablespoon milk

MAKES 2 SERVINGS

Place enough Brie on one bread slice to cover the entire slice. Cover Brie with sliced sundried peaches and press down. Top with another slice of bread. Spray a griddle with nonstick coating. Place the eggs in a shallow bowl and beat with the milk. Dip the bread package in the egg mixture on both sides, but do not soak. Quickly fry on both sides until golden. Cover the pan for a moment or two, to heat the sandwich through. (If you prefer the Brie runny, leave it on the heat just a minute or so longer.)

—THE BEAUFORT INN

PICTURE FACING CHAPTER OPENER: TOMATO-AND-ROSEMARY FRENCH TOAST, RECIPE ON PAGE 92

THE BOATHOUSE AT THE LODGE AT LAKE LURE

Adding biscuit mix, such as Bisquick, to a dipping batter will help the toast be puffier when done.

Apricot French Toast Nougats with Leeks and Gruyère Cheese

❧

Who said French toast has to be a sweet treat? I enjoy the variation of an egg-dipped bread dish with a touch of both—sweet and savory—such as this one. As with most French toast recipes, it is always a good idea to warm your serving plates. Although this has a hint of the Swiss Alps to it, it is the Sangre de Cristo Mountains of New Mexico that guests are surrounded by while enjoying this dish in the heart of old Santa Fe.

6	eggs
1/2	cup milk
8	(1-inch thick) slices stale French bread, cut into 2-inch squares
6	tablespoons butter, divided
1	medium leek (white and light green parts only), sliced
1	cup grated Gruyère cheese
1	cup apricot preserves

MAKES 6 SERVINGS

Begin by making the batter. Combine the eggs and the milk in a small bowl and beat well. Soak the bread cubes in the egg mixture, turning to coat evenly.

In a medium skillet, melt 3 tablespoons of the butter. Sauté the leeks until soft—about 6 minutes. When done, remove the leeks from the pan and add the remaining butter. Sauté the bread cubes, turning to lightly brown all sides. Return the leeks to the pan and toss with the French toast.

Divide the squares among 6 serving plates. Top immediately with the cheese and add a heaping spoonful of apricot preserves in the center of each plate.

—GRANT CORNER INN

If you're having a down day, make a reservation for a stay at a country inn. Those who answer the phones at inns are trained to give good feelings to the caller, so you're bound to get an uplift. I almost always get a pick-me-up when I call an inn.

Mozzarella-and-Ricotta-Filled Toast with Honey-Rum Sauce

⚭

The mixture of textures in this splendid toast—great for a brunch or lunch as well as breakfast—reminds me of Eureka Springs, where they serve this dish. Artists fill the area, making it a diverse and colorful region, which, like the French toast here, is layered with many contrasts. Begin preparing this dish a day ahead.

Guy or gal cook, wear your mother's or grandmother's apron once in a while, just to remind yourself of old-fashioned values that can still work today. If nothing else, the aprons will bring a smile to your face and anyone else who sees you.

Filling

1/4	cup dark rum
3/4	cup water
1/4	cup raisins
12	ounces Ricotta cheese
4	ounces Mozzarella cheese, grated

Sauce

1	cup maple syrup
1	cup honey
2	tablespoons dark rum
1	tablespoon vanilla extract

Toast and Batter

8	(1-inch thick) diagonal slices French bread
2	eggs, beaten
2	cups light cream
3	tablespoons Grand Marnier
1/8	teaspoon nutmeg

MAKES 4 SERVINGS

*B*egin preparing the filling a day ahead. In a small container, combine the rum and water. Add the raisins and soak them in the rum and water overnight in a refrigerator.

Next day, in a mixing bowl, combine the Ricotta and Mozzarella cheeses. Drain the raisins and add them to the cheese. Stir well to combine. Set aside and prepare the sauce.

Combine the maple syrup, honey, rum, and vanilla in a medium saucepan. Stir over low heat until warm and completely blended. Keep warm.

With a sharp knife, slit each bread slice lengthwise, through the crust, to form a pocket. Press about 4 tablespoons of the filling mixture into each bread pocket.

To make the batter, combine the eggs, cream, Grand Marnier, and nutmeg. Dip each filled bread slice into the batter, turning evenly to coat. On a lightly oiled griddle, sauté the slices over medium heat until browned on both sides.

—THE HEARTSTONE INN

Tomato-and-Rosemary French Toast with Cheese Sauce

⌒⌒

Great for breakfast or brunch, have fun interchanging the herbs and spices. Use whatever is fresh. I often use a crusty rosemary bread for this dish. But it is also delicious with sourdough or Italian bread.

"Mankind is divisible into two great classes—hosts and guests," wrote essayist Sir Max Beerbohm. What a way to explain this phenomenon we call bed-and-breakfast!

Sauce			1	large leaf sage, finely chopped
1	cup white sauce *		1	cup undiluted (canned) tomato soup
1	cup grated Asiago cheese (may substitute with Parmesan)		6	(1-inch) slices sourdough or other crusty bread
¹/₂	teaspoon dry mustard		2	tablespoons butter
¹/₈	teaspoon cayenne pepper			

Toast			Assembly	
3	eggs			Chopped fresh cilantro for garnish
¹/₄	cup milk			Chopped fresh chives for garnish
¹/₂	teaspoon white pepper			
1¹/₂	teaspoons chopped fresh rosemary			

MAKES 6 SERVINGS

*B*egin by making the cheese sauce. Heat the white sauce and stir in the grated cheese, stirring until incorporated. Add the mustard and cayenne. Keep warm.

Prepare the dipping batter. In a large bowl, beat the eggs and milk until well blended. Beat in the white pepper, rosemary, sage and soup. Heat a large skillet and melt the butter over medium-high heat. Dip the bread in the batter and sauté on the grill for a few minutes on both sides or until golden brown, cooking over medium heat.

Pool ¹/₄ cup of the cheese sauce off center on each serving plate. Place a piece of cooked bread in the center. Sprinkle fresh chives over all. Place a wisp of cilantro on the cheese sauce and serve. Pass extra cheese sauce around in a small pitcher.

* To make a cup of white sauce, make a roux of 2 tablespoons butter and 2 tablespoons all-purpose flour. Blend over low heat until thick and slowly stir in 1 cup of milk. Cook and stir constantly with a wooden spoon over moderate heat until thick and smooth, about 2 minutes.

—GAIL'S KITCHEN

[93]

Baked Ham and Swiss French Toast Casserole

વ∽**ળ**

Consider this make-ahead recipe for brunch or as the main course for a hearty break-fast with a side of sweet bread or muffins. Sometime, get out to this elegant inn sur-rounded by a charming town with lots of antiques-hunting nearby. You need to begin this recipe the night before.

1	cup finely chopped ham
1	cup grated Swiss cheese
1/4	cup mayonnaise
1/2	teaspoon non-grainy mustard
8	slices dense sandwich bread (such as Arnold Brick Oven)
6	eggs
1 1/4	cups milk

MAKES 4 SERVINGS

The night before serving: Combine the ham, cheese, mayonnaise, and mustard. Set aside. Lightly toast the bread in a toaster. Divide the ham mixture evenly over 4 slices of the bread. Top with the remaining 4 slices. Cut each sandwich diagonally into 4 triangles. In a well-greased 6x9x2-inch baking dish, stand each triangle upright on its outside edge, making 2 rows.

In a mixing bowl, beat the eggs and the milk and pour the mixture over the tri-angles. Cover and refrigerate overnight.

Next morning, preheat the oven to 325°. Bake the casserole, uncovered, for 35 minutes until set. Let the casserole stand about 5 to 10 minutes before serving. Slice between the sandwiches, and serve 3 or 4 triangles per person.

—BOYDVILLE, THE INN AT MARTINSBURG

A ROOM AWAITS GUESTS AT SETTLERS INN.

Pesto and Goat Cheese French Toast with Sundried Tomatoes

❧

Breakfast suits this dish just fine but it can be served anytime of day. The tangy sundried tomatoes and salty olives contrast the delicate goat cheese, while the pesto crowns the toast in perfect harmony. Use fresh-baked, crusty bread. If you were near the inn, you could purchase the bread there. It is some of the best I have ever tasted, baked by master baker Marcia Dunsmore who developed this recipe.

4	eggs
1	cups milk
6	slices Italian bread cut into 1-inch thick slices
3/4	cup goat cheese
1/3	cup chopped sundried tomatoes
1/4	cup chopped calamata olives
1/2	cup pesto sauce

MAKES 6 SERVINGS

*W*hisk eggs with the milk and set aside.

Cut the bread into pockets, by splitting down through the crust on the top of the bread with the tip of the knife. Do not cut all the way through the bread.

In a small bowl mix the goat cheese with the sundried tomatoes and the olives. Stuff each pocket with the sundried tomatoes and the olives. Stuff each pocket with the cheese mixture. Dip each pocket into the egg and milk mixture. Sauté in a skillet with a light coating of olive oil. over medium heat. Serve with a dollop of pesto sauce on top.

—THE SETTLERS INN

"A loaf of bread," the walrus said, "is what we chiefly need."—Lewis Carroll

Cornmeal-and-Black-Pepper-Bread French Toast with Garden Relish

✐⊙✐

Aside from breakfast, this French toast makes a delightful luncheon treat. The bread is perky with its peppery twist and is tamed by the cleansing relish with its fresh-from-the-garden ingredients. The unusual bread is one of baker Marcia Dunsmore's repertoire of homemade breads and makes a great accompaniment to other meals. Freeze any leftover bread.

Bread

1/4	cup honey
1	tablespoon plus 1 teaspoon yeast
1/2	cup water
1 1/3	cups buttermilk
1	cup cornmeal (stoneground preferred)
2	tablespoons corn oil
1	tablespoon plus 1 teaspoon salt
1	tablespoon plus 1 teaspoon cracked black pepper
5	cups all-purpose flour

Batter

4	eggs
1	cup milk

Relish

1	medium cucumber, seeded and cut into 1/4-inch dice
1	medium tomato, seeded and cut into 1/4-inch dice
1/2	medium red onion, finely chopped
1	tablespoon parsley
	Salt

Assembly

12	(1/2-inch thick) slices corn meal and black pepper bread
12	slices Monterey Jack or any soft mild cheese

MAKES 4 TO 6 SERVINGS

*P*reheat the oven to 350°. Blend together all the ingredients, except the flour, by hand or with a dough hook. When well blended, add the flour and knead by hand for about 8 minutes. Divide the dough in half. Shape into rounds and bake on a baking sheet for 40 minutes or until bread sounds hollow when tapped. Let bread cool and slice into 6 (1/2-inch) slices.

Whisk together the eggs and milk. Dip the bread slices into the egg batter and sauté the pieces on one side. Flip over and sauté on the other side, placing 2 slices of cheese on the cooked side to melt while the uncooked side sautés.

Mix together the ingredients for the relish adding salt to taste and serve a few tablespoons overtop two slices of bread per serving.

—THE SETTLERS INN

Directory

The Bailiwick Inn
4023 Chain Bridge Road
Fairfax, VA 22030
(703) 691-2266

Rooms: 14

An exquisitely appointed urban
Colonial inn where every guest room is
named and decorated with a Virginia-
born statesman (including four presidents)
in mind.

The Beaufort Inn
809 Port Republic St.
Beaufort, South Carolina 29902
(803) 521-9000

Rooms: 11

Southern hospitality and elegance
abound at this 1907 inn at the center of
Beaufort's Historic Landmark District.

Beckmann Inn
222 East Guenther St.
San Antonio, TX 78204
(210) 229-1449

Rooms: 5

An 1886 home in San Antonio's King
William Historical District with both
Victorian and Greek Revival influences.

Blue Harbor House
67 Elm St.
Camden, ME 04843
(207) 236-3196

Rooms: 10

Close to both the mountains and the
sea, this restored 1810 Cape Cod is decorated with country antiques and quilts.

Boydville, The Inn at Martinsburg
601 South Queen St.
Martinsburg, WV 25401
(304) 263-1448

Rooms: 6

An 1812 stone plantation home, brimming with Civil War history.

Canyon Villa
125 Canyon Circle Drive
Sedona, AZ 86351
(520) 284-1226

Rooms: 11

If "a room with a view" is what you crave, then most any one of the guest accommodations will thrill you here at this B&B amid Sedona's amazing red rock formations.

The Chicago Pike Inn
215 East Chicago St.
Coldwater, MI 49036
(517) 279-8744

Rooms: 6

A stately 1903 masterpiece of Colonial Reform architecture with a grand staircase of cherry hardwoods that leads up to a beautiful stained-glass window and the guest rooms beyond.

Clifton Country Inn
Route 13
Charlottesville, VA 22901
(804) 971-1800

Rooms: 14

Once the home of Thomas Jefferson's daughter, this Colonial gem of an inn is just a stone's throw from the third president's Monticello estate.

Corner George Inn
Corner of Main & Mill
Maeystown, IL 62256
(618) 458-6660

Rooms: 5

Ask how the inn got its name from a former resident of this quaint Midwest village settled by German immigrants in 1852.

Doanleigh Wallagh Inn
217 E. 37th St.
Kansas City, MO 64111
(816) 753-2667

Rooms: 9

Two 1907 homes furnished with antiques and overlooking Hyde Park.

The French Manor
Route 191 South
Huckleberry Road
South Sterling, PA 18460
(717) 676-3244

Rooms: 9

Art aficionado Joseph Hirshhorn modeled this stunning house after his French manor in the south of France. Soaring architecture, picturesque vistas, cozy gourmet dinners by the fire, and luxurious guest rooms spell romance European style.

The Gingerbread Mansion Inn
400 Berding Street
P.O. Box 40
Ferndale, CA 95540
(707) 786-4000

Rooms: 11

This enchanting mansion looks as if it was taken straight out of a fairy tale. Live happily ever after for a few days while enjoying a fireside bubble bath, bedside chocolates and afternoon tea. It is deserving of all the recognition it receives worldwide.

Grant Corner Inn
122 Grant Ave.
Santa Fe, NM 87501
(505) 983-6678

Rooms: 13

A restored Colonial-style home just two blocks from Santa Fe's bustling plaza.

The Heartstone Inn
35 Kingshighway
Eureka Springs, AR 72631
(501) 253-8916

Rooms: 14

Enjoy the nostalgic charms of this restored Victorian at the center of Eureka Springs and all its artsy activities and attractions.

Howard Creek Ranch
40501 North Highway One
Westport, CA 95488
(707) 964-6725

Rooms: 8

A late-1800s farmhouse on a 20-acre ranch with views of the Pacific and the mountains...and the beach is just 100 yards away.

Inn at the Round Barn Farm
R.R. 1, Box 247
East Warren Road
Waitsfield, VT 05673
(802) 496-2276

Rooms: 11

The 1910 round barn—saved and restored by the innkeepers—is just one of the irresistible attractions of this luxurious inn on 85 rolling Vermont country acres.

The Lodge on Lake Lure
Route 1, Box 529A
Lake Lure, NC 28691
(704) 625-2789

Rooms: 11

You'll find a cozy hunting lodge atmos-
phere here plus incredible views of a very
special Blue Ridge Mountain lake.

Manor House Inn
612 Hughes Street
Cape May, NJ 08204
(609) 884-4710

Rooms: 10

A perfect base for Cape May's lively
activities from carriage and trolley tours to
whale or bird watching and, of course,
beach-going.

Maplewood Inn
Route 22-A South
Fair Haven, VT 05743
(802) 265-8039

Rooms: 5

An 1843 Greek Revival inn on
Vermont's historic register with its own
antique shop plus bikes and a canoe for
guests.

Meadowlark Manor
241 West 9th Ave.
Red Cloud, NE 68970
(402) 746-3550

Rooms: 4

A historic manor replete with antique
Victorian lighting and soft flowered carpets.

My Blue Heaven
1041 5th St.
Pawnee City, NE 68420
(402) 852-3131

Rooms: 2

A 1920s home decorated with antiques, quilts, and tatting.

North Garden Inn
1014 North Garden
Bellingham, WA 98225
(360) 671-7828

Rooms: 10

Several guest rooms boast views of Bellingham Bay and the Northwest's stunning summer sunsets at this Queen Anne Victorian on the National Historic Register.

Prescott Pines Inn
901 White Spar Road
Prescott, AZ 86303
(602) 445-7270

Rooms: 13

The 1902 two-story main house and four separate guest houses all reflect the inn's country Victorian comforts.

Ravenscroft Inn
533 Quincy St.
Port Townsend, WA 98368
(360) 385-2784

Rooms: 9

A Colonial-style seaport inn located on the Olympic Peninsula.

The Settlers Inn
Four Main Avenue
Hawley, PA 18428
(717) 226-2993

Rooms: 18

Some of the best food in the country is
served here. The inn cooks with locally
grown organic ingredients. The menu is
uplifting, creative, and memorable. Rooms
are simple and all different—ranging from
floral prints and wicker to all-white rooms
with only touches of color and rooms that
host old-fashioned beds and reminders of
an era when one stayed at a place for a few
weeks at a time.

Seven Sisters Inn
820 Southeast Fort King St.
Ocala, FL 34471
(904) 867-1170

Rooms: 7

Sip raspberry tea on the veranda, enjoy
flowering walkways or play croquet on the
lawn at this meticulously restored 1888
Queen Anne Victorian in the heart of
Ocala's historic district.

The Shelburne Inn
Pacific Highway 103 & 45th St.
Seaview, WA 98644
(360) 642-2442

Rooms: 13 rooms; 2 suites

Art Nouveau stained-glass windows
brighten this inn, and a 28-mile strip of
wild Pacific coastline is only a 10-minute
walk away.

Turtleback Farm Inn
Route 1, Box 650
Eastsound, WA 98245
(360) 376-4914

Rooms: 7

A country farmhouse on Orcas Island in
Puget Sound that makes an ideal base for
hiking, biking, fishing, sea kayaking, boat-
ing, and much more.

Victorian Treasure B&B
115 Prairie Street
Lodi, WI 53555
(608) 592-5199

Rooms: 11

Luxurious bed-and-breakfast in a tiny town with streets as you remember them. Todd Seidl, owner and innkeeper, knows how to cook, and it shows on a sumptuous breakfast table. One of America's truest and finest B&Bs.

The Woolverton Inn
6 Woolverton Road
Stockton, NJ 08559
(609) 397-0802

Rooms: 13

Dramatic Victorian with decidedly mansard roof. Gardens are splendid and the walk to town delightful. Rooms have trompe l'oeil flowers. Breakfast by candlelight.

Index